THIRTEEN ROCKS

DR. PAM OGDIN-ROSEMIER

authorHOUSE®

AuthorHouse™ LLC
1663 Liberty Drive
Bloomington, IN 47403
www.authorhouse.com
Phone: 1-800-839-8640

Published by AuthorHouse   08/27/2014

ISBN: 978-1-4969-3575-5 (sc)
ISBN: 978-1-4969-3559-5 (e)

KJV
Scripture quotations marked KJV are from the Holy Bible, King James Version
(Authorized Version). First published in 1611. Quoted from the KJV Classic
Reference Bible, Copyright © 1983 by The Zondervan Corporation.

FOREWORD

To Parents and Friends,

This story is a ceremony about a rite of passage and is meant to honor anyone beginning a new experience such as a birthday, graduation, promotion, or even a wedding.

This ceremony can easily be adapted to suit individual needs as it encourages the one being honored to walk from person to person with a backpack filled with 13 rocks. If a backpack is unavailable, use a brown paper bag, a box, or a pillowcase filled with 13 objects such as 13 Legos or 13 buttons. The number of objects, of course, will vary depending on your special occasion. The idea is to let relatives and friends share a family tradition, a blessing, or even advice as each one symbolically removes an object from the backpack, box, bag, or pillowcase. This simple gesture is meant to show the honoree that he or she is special, is loved, and has the support of family and friends through the journey of life.

Your ceremony can take place on a beach, in a park, backyard, even in a living room. It is my prayer that this rite of passage will bring joy not only to the person being honored, but also to those who participate in this simple ceremony.

Dr. Pam Ogdin-Rosemier

Thirteen Rocks

PROLOGUE

This is a story of a child, one mountain and thirteen rocks.

With an inquiring look at her son, Mother asked, "Are you sure you still want to do this? I know you are thirteen years old today, but this mountain is a challenge, even for an adult to climb." Looking through the window, Mother thought the mountain appeared so large and Child seemed so small.

"Yes, I am sure. But Dad promised," whined Child. "He said he would be here to watch me climb the mountain for my birthday today."

"I know," said Mother. "I am certain he would be here if he could."

Following breakfast, as Mother watched Child put on a warm jacket and cap, she began to tell again the legend of the Mountain. "In ancient times, the Israelites disobeyed the instructions of God, so it took them 40 years instead of 15 days to walk around the mountain. Only the children of the lost generation were allowed into the Promised Land. Legend says that if a child can carry a backpack filled with thirteen heavy rocks to the top of the mountain, then it is no longer a child, but a young adult who has learned the lessons of the mountain on how to honor and obey God."

With the help of Mother, Child slid thin arms through the straps of the very heavy backpack and almost fell over backwards. Then Child took a final look around the cozy kitchen. There was a beautifully decorated birthday cake with thirteen candles on the dining table just waiting to be cut later. Surrounding the cake were thirteen birthday presents in every hue of the rainbow.

With excitement that reached far inside his stomach, Child knew that this birthday was going to be the best one ever! Child turned, looked at Mother, and gave a final wave.

Mother smiled, nodded her head in encouragement, and said a small prayer as Child set off alone to conquer the mountain.

CHAPTER 1

T

In the beginning, the pathway up the mountain was clear and the climb was not very steep. The day was lemonade sunny and sunglasses bright and the sky was the color of a flock of blue jays. Child smiled and said aloud, "This is going to be easy."

But soon, Child had to stop and catch his breath. The mountain path had gradually disappeared, the trail ahead seemed suddenly much steeper than before, and the backpack was so much heavier. Silently Child said, "I will not let this mountain defeat me! I will climb to the top and today I will become a young adult." Child took a deep breath and continued to slowly make his way up the side of the mountain.

After a few hours of climbing, the day had become less sunny, the sky had changed to the color of gravel and there were low clouds all around. Child was only one fourth of the way up the mountain and had to pause to catch his breath.

Refusing to be defeated, this time Child said out loud, "I will not let this mountain defeat me. I will climb to the top and today I will become a young adult." Child then pulled on the straps of his backpack to help shift the weight of the thirteen heavy rocks and began to climb again.

Halfway up the mountain now, Child felt like quitting. His legs had grown weary and the rocks inside the backpack had become burdensome.

Needing a break, Child sat down heavily on a large jagged boulder and stared up at the ominous mountain. The mountain appeared so much bigger than before and was now covered in a fine mist that felt cool on Child's hot, sweaty face. Suddenly, with new determination, Child shouted at the top of his voice, "I will not let this mountain defeat me!" I will climb to the top and today I will become a young adult."

Once again, Child struggled up the mountain, cold, tired, and a little fearful that the mountain may indeed win the battle. Suddenly, Child remembered to do something he should have done at the bottom of the mountain.

Child asked for help. Child bowed his head, put his hands together, and said a short, silent prayer. "Dear Lord, please help me to carry this heavy load to the top of the mountain so today, I can become a young adult. Amen."

Child expected an instant miracle and waited for God to send an angel to convey it to the top of the mountain or, at least, to make the mountain less steep. But nothing happened. Nothing at all. So Child repeated his prayer out loud. "Dear Lord, please help me to carry this heavy load to the top of the mountain so today, I can become a young adult. Amen." Child waited but still, nothing happened.

Finally, Child stood up and said, "I will try one last time to carry this heavy load by myself to the top of the mountain so today, I can become a young adult."

Child was breathing harder now and sweating inside his coat. His legs felt like lead and his back and arms ached but Child lowered his head and concentrated on putting one foot in front of another. The mountain had become too steep, the air had turned cold, and Child was so very, very tired.

After hours of climbing, Child could go no further. He stumbled and fell down hard with the thirteen rocks on his back.

Child knew with a sickening dread that he would not make it to the top of the mountain. With a final sigh, Child buried his head in his folded arms, and began to cry. Child continued to sob and wondered how to face family and friends with such a defeat.

As Child lay on the cold, hard ground, he remembered an earlier conversation with Dad.

"Why don't I just pretend to climb the mountain? No one has to know I never made it to the top." Dad's reply was still strong inside his head.

"That would be a lie, and more than disappointing God by lying to others, you would be lying to yourself. Inside, you would always know the truth. As an adult, we live most of our lives in the valleys. Occasionally, a mountain is put in our way to make us stronger. If we are brave enough to climb that mountain, we will have a magnificent view of the whole valley below. Even though the air is too thin to live permanently on the top of the mountain, the vista is worth the climb. To be an adult is to accept both the valleys and the mountain climbs, and appreciate the view after we get there."

Child lay defeated on the cold, unyielding ground for a very long time.

Suddenly, something touched Child's shoulder and someone said his name. Startled, Child looked up and saw a miracle. Kneeling down was Child's Best Friend in the whole world. "How is this possible?" Child thought.

Best Friend said, "I have been waiting for you to come around this side of the mountain and to give you this envelope." Best Friend handed the envelope to Child who took it with a puzzled look. The envelope was very plain but had a beautifully monogrammed "T" on the outside. Opening it, Child pulled out the note inside. This is what it said:

"TRUST God who can do all things!"

Best Friend then helped Child to stand and said, "God has answered your prayer and has sent me to help you. We can do this together."

Then Best Friend did something quite unexpected. It lifted the flap of Child's backpack and removed one of the thirteen rocks.

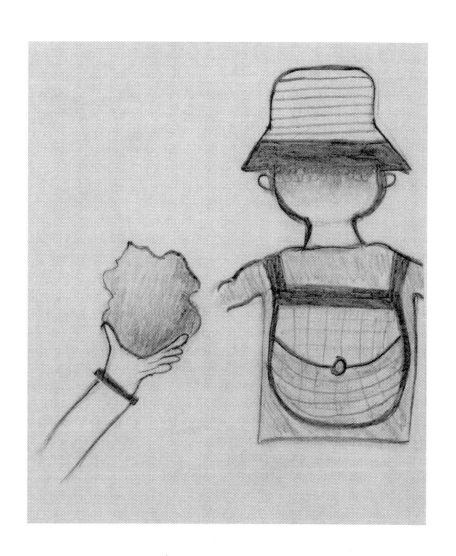

CHAPTER 2

The two children struggled up the mountain and were getting very tired when they suddenly heard a cheerful voice say, "Hello, I have been waiting for you!"

Child blinked hard, but there leaning against a giant boulder, was Youth Leader from church. Youth Leader said, "I am here to give you this." He held out an envelope with the letter "H" on it. Child took the envelope, opened it, and read:

> "HONOR God at all times, He will take care of you. He
> will not always remove your mountains, but He will help
> you find a way to the top of them. Always remember what
> it says in Ecclesiastes 4:9,12. A person standing alone can
> be attacked and defeated, but two can stand back to back
> and conquer. Three is even better, for a triple braided cord
> is not easily broken."

Child felt something more inside the envelope. Turning it upside down, an object fell into Child's hand. It was a simple triple-braided cord bracelet which Child easily slipped over his wrist.

Youth Leader and Best Friend admired the bracelet and then Youth Leader opened Child's backpack and removed one of the rocks and said, "I will carry this one for you."

So off they went, all three, arm in arm as a triple-braided cord, to continue climbing the mountain.

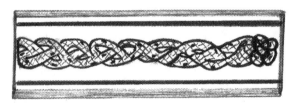

Ecclesiastes 4:9

CHAPTER 3

I

After scrambling over stones and brush that looked like dried broccoli, the trio noticed the landscape had changed. Now there were odd trees shaped like monsters and ghouls anticipating a march in a Halloween parade. Suddenly, Child stopped in amazement.

"Grand-dad!" Child shouted. "How did you get up here on this mountain?"

Grand-dad replied, "I have been waiting for you. With that, he handed Child another envelope, this time with the letter "I" on the outside. While Grand-dad, Youth Leader, and Best Friend were talking and sharing their experiences, Child opened the envelope and read:

INTEGRITY is always speaking the truth and doing what is right, even if it is not popular."

Grand-dad then came over to Child and said, "Are you all right?"

Child replied, "I will not lie to you Grand-dad. There were a couple of times when I felt like quitting but two friends showed up to help me along the way."

Grand-dad said, "You have shown integrity by speaking the truth. There will always be those who just pretend to climb the mountain but an honorable young adult will never lie or cheat and will always give its best effort. That is why I know you will make it to the top!" Grand-dad smiled, opened Child's backpack, and removed one of the rocks. "I will be glad to carry this one for you."

As they all continued up the mountain, each carrying a rock, Child was surprised that the climb, although still difficult, seemed so much easier with four people and only ten rocks in the backpack.

CHAPTER 4

R

Older Brother had been waiting patiently in the shadow of the mountain for a very long time. At first, Child did not see him until Older Brother began to playfully shadow box around The Group. Older Brother beamed and playfully pulled an envelope with the letter R from his jacket pocket. Using his hands, Older Brother signed, "I have been waiting for you!"

Eagerly looking inside, Child knew by now that these messages were answers to prayer. This message was brief and read:

"RESPECT everyone, even if he or she is different or weaker."

Child read the message again and then looked over at Older Brother and smiled. Older Brother stood there with his spikey hair, loud clothes, signing to Grand-dad, Youth Leader, and Best Friend. He had been born deaf but that did not stop the exuberance Older Brother showed for living. Older Brother signed on Sundays during the Praise Service and Child loved him just the way he was.

Older Brother caught his eye and came over to Child. He signed with his hands, "I will carry one of these for you!" He then lifted the flap on the backpack, and as the others had done before, removed one of the rocks.

CHAPTER 5

T

Over the next few hours, Child and The Group were to meet many more friends and relatives. Not too far ahead, Child was pleasantly surprised to see Next Door Neighbor. Child remembered how kind he was to fix a broken bicycle and to pump up a deflated soccer ball. Next Door Neighbor smiled and said, "I am so glad to see you. I have been waiting to give you your next envelope. The envelope looked like all the others but had a large block "T" on the outside. The inside message read,

"THANKFULLNESS in all things!"

Child had been taught to say, "Please" and "Thank You" but this message meant being thankful, not just for the good things, but the bad things too. As Child pondered that, he thought Dad would probably say it this way, "Be thankful for the valleys AND the mountains."

Next Door Neighbor bent down and with those skillful hands removed one of the remaining rocks from the backpack. "I will carry this one for you!"

CHAPTER 6

E

With Child and his backpack in the lead, The Group continued its slow climb up the mountain. There, waiting around the next bend was Grandmother. She always smelled of vanilla which was probably one of the reasons Grand-dad was always giving her kisses on the cheek. Grandmother accepted Grand-dad's kiss in greeting and then, with outstretched arms, drew Child to her and said, "You are my favorite grandchild and I have been waiting to give this to you." She reached inside her apron pocket under her overcoat and produced an envelope that smelled like sugar cookies and labeled with the letter "E". Inside, the message read,

"ENJOY life with a positive attitude."

Still in Grandmother's embrace, Child felt her reach inside his backpack to remove one of the remaining rocks. Grandmother whispered, "I will carry this one for you."

As Grand-dad reached for Grandmother's hand, Child smiled and looked at The Group. The mountain might be getting higher but so were Child's spirits because he felt loved. Perhaps Grandmother was right. A positive attitude can make any bad situation better. For the first time, Child realized he was actually enjoying the climb up this mountain.

CHAPTER 7

E

The Group carefully stayed on the mountain path because the wind was strong, the air was thin, and the forest on the mountain had become very dark and dense. No longer shrubs and low bushes but giant trees with outstretched branches extended to the sky as if in exuberant joy.

As The Group stopped to rest, they were amazed to see a jogger coming down the mountain toward them. Child recognized him immediately. It was School Coach who was waving enthusiastically at The Group. He jogged over and addressed Child. "I have been waiting to give this special envelope to you." The envelope was the same as all the others but Child was surprised to see that there was another "E" on the outside. Inside, Child read the shortest message yet:

"ENCOURAGE all!"

Child must have looked puzzled because School Coach said, "I have noticed that you are always there to help your team mates play their best and you even come early to help them practice. A young adult is never too big or too busy to inspire others to achieve their goals. So I am here today to encourage you!"

School Coach then opened Child's backpack, removed one of the remaining rocks, and vigorously declared, "I will carry this one for you!"

CHAPTER 8

N

"Who would they meet next on this mountain path?" Child wondered.

This day had certainly taken many turns, and just like the path they were on, filled with many surprises. Child was the first to see Uncle sitting on a fallen log. After greeting The Group, Uncle said to Child, "I am so proud that you have made it this far. You have a family who loves you, you have many friends, you are healthy, and have talents that make you unique."

Uncle then handed Child an envelope with the letter "N" on the outside. Child tried to think of words that began with the letter "N" in anticipation of opening this new envelope. Could it be "Notable?" "Normal?" "Numerous?" There was only one way to find out so Child quickly opened the flap and pulled out the card. This is what it said:

"NUMBER your blessings. Remember God loves you and has provided these blessings to make you happy."

Uncle gave a short nod, turned, and removed one of the rocks from the backpack and said, "I will carry this one for you!"

A journey which had begun with one person, had now grown to a small band of nine.

CHAPTER 9

R

The Group had not gone far when they stopped because they heard someone singing and the echo was repeating far down into the valley below. The voice was pure and strong and the man Child saw in the path ahead was no stranger to miracles. Pastor's face broke into a wide smile when he said, "I have been waiting for you!"

By this time, Child knew there was an envelope and so with outstretched hand he took it, observed the letter "R" on the outside, opened it, and read with a quizzical look one solitary word:

"REWARDS"

Pastor explained. "I have watched you share when the offering plate goes by on Sunday mornings, and have noticed that you are never reluctant to ask for forgiveness if you think you have made someone else unhappy. A godly young adult will always find a way to generously share its time and resources with others. Even if no one else sees what you have done, God will know, and will reward you my child."

As he spoke, Pastor removed one more rock from the backpack and declared, "I will carry this one for you!"

The climb was getting much steeper now but Child's backpack was so much lighter, thanks to family and friends. Deep in his heart, Child immediately knew he would make it to the top of the mountain.

CHAPTER 10

O

A girl from school was the next person waiting on the mountain trail. Girl was shy and said sincerely, "I really like the way you play your guitar. You are always so eager to play whenever anyone asks you. I especially like to hear you play in the Praise Band at church because it makes singing the songs so much fun. All of the kids at school have different talents. Some of them are creative with their hands, some are good with numbers or words, others excel in sports or play the guitar like you do." Girl handed Child an envelope she had been holding. She said, "I wonder why it has an "O" on the outside?" When Child opened it, they read together:

"ONE TALENT. A young adult will always strive to find that One Talent that sets him or her apart from everyone else."

"That seems like really good advice," stated Girl. Then she removed one of the remaining rocks from Child's backpack and kindly said, "I will carry this one for you."

CHAPTER 11

C

As The Group struggled higher toward the peak of the mountain, Child was actually looking forward to seeing the next miracle and with each step tried to anticipate just who it would be waiting for them. As they slowly made their way around the side of the mountain, Child was not disappointed to see Favorite Aunt. She was so pretty and full of life. Favorite Aunt said, "I have been waiting for you and am so excited to see you. You have almost made it to the top of the mountain." Favorite Aunt then handed a new envelope to Child. This envelope was like all the others, plain but, in this case, had a beautiful illuminated letter "C" like you would find in the Book of Kells.

The Group sat down while Child pulled out a sheet of paper to read the following:

"CONSEQUENCES"

"Everything we do in life has consequences. That is why making a mistake or failing is not always a bad thing. Sometimes we learn more from those things that do not work. A young adult must learn to accept the consequences of bad decisions and appreciate the blessing from good ones. This is not always easy but strive to do what you think is best for yourself, your family, and your friends, and you will be blessed. Always work hard and expect good things to happen."

When Child finished reading, the paper was returned to the envelope like all the others and Child took a moment to contemplate. Child looked at The Group who was busy laughing and talking and thought, "If not for them, I could not be here. I am blessed!"

Favorite Aunt looked around, stood up, and came over to Child. She opened the flap to the backpack and removed one of the remaining rocks. With pride written all over her face, she said, "I will carry this one for you."

Excitement was building as The Group got to its feet because they were almost to the top of the mountain. "Just a few more steps," Child thought, "and I will become a young adult."

CHAPTER 12

K

As The Group continued to climb, suddenly the sun broke through the mist and everyone came to an abrupt halt behind Child. They had made it to the top of the mountain. Everyone cheered and patted each other on the back. Grand-dad planted a kiss on Grandmother's cheek and Child turned toward a familiar voice.

"Mother!" Child shouted excitedly. "This is great! How did you get here before me?" The words came spilling out like Legos from an open box. "Wait until I tell you what has happened to me today! You won't believe it!"

Mother was beaming as she hugged Child and said, "I know! I have been waiting for you to give you this envelope." Child drank in the perfumed scent of Mother as he opened the envelope with a "K" This is what it said inside:

"KNOW that you are always loved. Just as God loves each one of us, I will always love you."

Child looked around at Mother and The Group and could not remember ever being this happy. There were two remaining rocks in Child's backpack. Mother came over and took the next to the last rock out. This left just one rock. Child expected Mother to remove the last rock too but she did not. Puzzled, Child just stood there until Mother explained. "Sometimes, you have to carry the final rock for yourself. No one else can do it for you as much as they would like to."

"I understand," said Child. It is this rock that makes us strong." Mother smiled and knew in her heart that today, at this moment, Child had become Young Adult.

Young Adult then took each of the envelopes and positioned them in a smooth place on the ground. Young Adult was careful to place each one in the order received. It had one envelope for each of the twelve rocks family and friends had removed from the backpack. Too bad there was not a final envelope for the last rock.

CHAPTER 13

S

Just as Young Adult was trying to think of a way to preserve this wonderful moment, a tall man in a military uniform stepped out from behind The Group.

"Dad? DAD!" Young Adult shouted and launched himself through the air and into Dad's outstretched arms. "I was disappointed this morning when you were not here for my birthday. I am so glad to see you!"

Dad said, "I promised you I would be here and I like to keep my promises if I can. I knew you could do it! I have been waiting here for you because I was certain that you would not give up. Young adults should always persevere in their relationships, their jobs, and in their willingness to serve God." Dad released Young Adult who smiled at the letter "S" on the final envelope.

"SERVE God, your family, your country, and your friends with a cheerful spirit!"

Dad said, "I love the way you encourage your brothers and sisters. You help them with their school work and always make time to play with them. I appreciate the way you are respectful to me and your mother and help out around the house with your chores. I love the times that we get to spend together because I enjoy being around you." Dad took a loving look at Mother and continued, "We are blessed to have you for our child. Happy Birthday Young Adult!"

Then Dad opened the flap to the backpack and removed the final rock. He gently placed it into the hands of Young Adult and said, "Today, you are no longer a child but a young adult of whom I am very proud."

CHAPTER 14

All the time Dad had been talking, The Group had been stacking their stones on top of one another. As Mother, Dad, and Young Adult walked over to add the last two rocks to the pile, they heard Pastor say, "These stones are very important."

In I Peter 2:1-9, St. Peter explains that once the Holy Spirit dwells inside us, we become living stones in a spiritual house where Jesus is the cornerstone. Let these rocks become a monument for others who climb the mountain so they will ask, 'What are these rocks?' And we can tell them of our struggle here today and God's grace so they may know that the Lord is God."

Young Adult bowed his head and silently prayed, "Lord, please help me to be a living stone so when others ask me what these stones mean, I can tell them what You have done for me today. Amen."

Together, The Group looked out over the valley they loved and realized that today was a very special day, not just for Young Adult, but for all of them. They were all reminded what it means to be a responsible adult.

CHAPTER 15

"So, what do you think?" said Dad to Young Adult. "Today, you are no longer 12 but 13 years old." Young Adult thought for a moment and then placed the last envelope on the ground next to all the others. Young Adult saw what it spelled out and turned toward Mother and Dad and replied, "I have learned that life is not always going to be easy. There will be many mountains for me to climb. But if I:

T rust and
H onor God, have
I ntegrity, show
R espect, am
T hankful,
E njoy life,
E ncourage others,
N umber my blessings, enjoy my

R ewards, find my
O ne true talent, accept the
C onsequences,
K now I am loved, and
S erve God, then I am assured He will send help along the way.

"What do I think? I think being 12 was really good."

Then stepping away from The Group, Young Adult pulled the cap off his head and with arms extended to the Heavens, shouted at the top of his voice. As it echoed from the top of the mountain, they all heard Young Adult say,

"BUT THIRTEEN ROCKS!"

Printed in the United States
By Bookmasters